Life's
SIX
Buckets

The Fulfillment Source Code: Human Edition

SAM GOODMAN

ISBN: 978-1-7340675-0-7

Good morning Gorgeous
☼ ♥ ☺

To Sophie:
I love ya kiddo.

You inspire me
You challenge me
You make me laugh
Being your dad is the greatest adventure
Thank you

ACKNOWLEDGMENTS

- Thank you to the hundreds of scientists, the researchers, the technologists, the teachers, and the presenters. (Sources at back)

- Shout out to The Compilers, those podcasts are largely responsible for introducing me to the brainiacs above. Tim Ferriss, Joe Rogan, Tom Bilyeu, Shane Parrish...

- Thank you to my friends and family who have supported me, encouraged me, and endured me.

In this book, you may recognize inspirations from Abraham Maslow or Simon Sinek, but you probably won't recognize the subtle influences of my daughter, my mother, my sister or friends. They are all in here.

Thank you

PLEASE NOTE

This book represents about one-third of the first class of the Fulfillment Source Code course.

Easily, 98% of the content of the FSC course, comes from someone else; someone far smarter than me. What started as something for my daughter, has turned into a mission to help educate and empower kids everywhere.

I don't want to make a dent in the universe; I'd just like to fix a few.

Hope this helps.

TABLE OF CONTENT

APPENDICES

CHAPTER 1

THE $100,000,000 QUESTION

All right, everybody, gather round. I have a secret to share. Something your parents probably don't know yet; something that has taken years to discover and the effort of some of the world's brightest minds.

I'm totally serious.

But first, let's play a game!

Today, we're meeting our long-lost Uncle Joe.

Our Uncle Joe has left us some money and it looks like quite a bit of money.

What are we going to do with it?

First, let's read the letter that Uncle Joe left us:

Hi Kiddo,

Sorry I didn't get to spend as much time as I wanted with you. All right, to be honest, we never met. But I wish that we had.

Oh yeah, and I am leaving you my fortune.

To be precise, I am leaving you my entire fortune of $100.000.000.

Much love

Your very own uncle Joe

Wait a minute. Did I say "quite a bit" of money?

I mean, a TON OF MONEY! Uncle Joe was loaded!

One hundred million dollars! That's a fortune!

But what will you do with it?

I'll tell you what: write down the first two or three things that come to your mind when you imagine a whole truckload of money. So much money you could do almost anything.

Go on, write them down and we'll go from there.

Remember, there are no wrong answers, so write down the first two or three things that you think of.

So, let's see what we have here...

I want _____	I want _____	I want _____

Are you done? Did you go crazy?

I bought an island. Sorry, but not sorry.

I want an island!

What three things did YOU writedown that you'd buy right away with Uncle Joe's fortune?

Wow. That's interesting! Now, take a moment and think...

WHY did you want those things?

Remember, there are no right or wrong answers.

For each item on your list, write down why you chose to purchase this thing or experience, or why you chose to give it to a person or group.

_____ I want an island!	I want _____ _____ _____ _____ _____	I want _____ _____ _____ _____ _____	I want _____ _____ _____ _____ _____
Because of beach, ocean, Sunshine, and friends	Because _____ _____ _____ _____	Because _____ _____ _____ _____	Because _____ _____ _____ _____

I chose an island for myself because I have always wanted to wake up by the beach, jump into the ocean right away and enjoy the sunshine while hanging out with my friends.

Just don't mention sharks, okay?

Thanks.

All right, all right. Let's get down to business, shall we?
Last question, I promise.

Take another moment and think:

WHY did you want those things?

Again, there are no wrong answers.

I want _____ an island!	I want _____	I want _____	I want _____
Because of the beach, ocean, Sunshine, and friends	Because _____	Because _____	Because _____
I want that because sharing good times is awesome	And I want that because _____	And I want that because _____	And I want that because _____

Let's also answer questions about the three things we chose in the following manner:

I want ___a desert island___ because I will have a lot of fun swimming and enjoying the sunshine with my friends and I want that because sharing good times with friends and family is awesome

13

I want _____ because _____
and I want that because _____

I want _____ because _____
and I want that because _____

I want _____ because _____
and I want that because _____

How did it go? Let's take a look.

That's great. You all did a great job with this.

Those three things you chose each fit into a bucket. A what?

That's right, a bucket.

14

CHAPTER 2

YOU ARE A UNIQUE HUMAN

Just in case I lost you with the bucket, let me quickly say one thing I know for certain, even though we have never met: I know you are a unique human.

I couldn't possibly comment on your unique parts, because there is no way I could know enough about you, about where or how you grew up or about your family or friends. But I do know one thing for certain - you are human.

And just as gravity affects us all, whether we know about it or not, so too are there some things that all human beings have in common.

Every one of us, each human being, has six buckets; our buckets being the WHYS of life.

Something we all share because genetically, we're 99.9% identical!

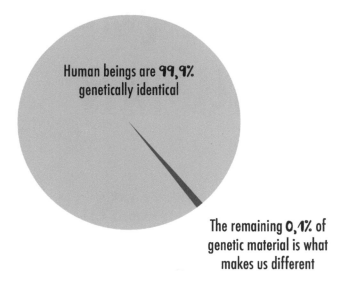

Human beings are **99,9%** genetically identical

The remaining **0,1%** of genetic material is what makes us different

We humans are far more similar than we are different.

When we realize our basic humanity and our shared needs, we grow closer and increase our understanding of how to lead better and more fulfilled lives.

CHAPTER 3

LIFE'S WHAT + HOW + WHY

What makes us unique may be the order of your buckets. Some of us prefer 2-3 buckets over the rest.

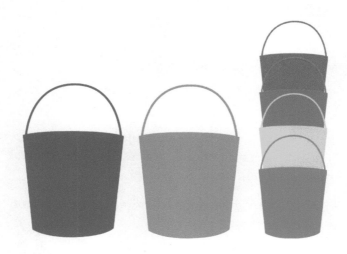

The **HOW** you live your life, your culture or religion may be different and the **WHAT** you do to fill your buckets, that's uniquely yours.

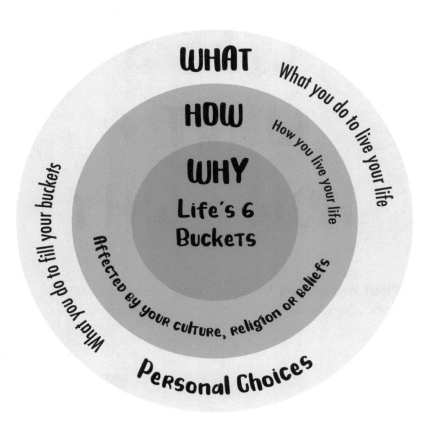

Around the world, different cultures and religions have grown over time as the people (families, tribes, etc) from that area sought out ways to fill their buckets.

So, what are those buckets? And what do we put inside them?

CHAPTER 4

YOUR SIX BUCKETS

SAFETY

We all want to feel safe and sound, and this bucket is where we do or put things that make us feel safe and secure.

Some people feel safe with lots of money in the bank, having a home, a secure job.

Others may enjoy learning skills to help them cope with danger, while others choose to avoid dangerous places and things.

What makes you feel safe?

What are some things you like to do to feel safe?

To feel safe I like to

FUN

Everyone likes to have fun, right? We love to feel good and enjoy life with friends and activities. There are many, many books written about all the various things people can do to feel good and have fun.

From reading a book, to eating rich chocolate fudge, to skydiving.

Everyone has their own favorite way. To do this, some of us just need to learn how to relax and hang out.

What are some things you like to do or have to help you feel good and have fun?

To have fun I like to

SIGNIFICANCE

What does this mean? Well, we all want to feel like we matter. Like we're seen. That in this big wide world someone notices us and says, "Hey, I see you. You matter. You're important".

There are many ways to fill this bucket: being a valued friend, family member, or contributing to a team or community. Other people matter, and they matter to us.

Sometimes adding value to others is actually the best way to fill our own buckets.

What are some things you like to do to help you feel significant?

To feel significant I like to

CONNECTIONS

Humans are social animals. We all need to feel that we belong, that we are loved and connected with our friends and family.

This bucket is for those you care about.

26

Always make the effort and take time for them, and in turn, they will do the same for you. We are hardwired for physical contact and face-to-face interaction, something screens, on their own, can NOT deliver.

What are some things you like to do to help you feel connected?

To feel connected I like to

5

GROWTH

What does this mean? It means improvement. We all want to feel like we're becoming a better version of ourselves. It means turning a dream into a goal and working toward it.

Growth can occur in many ways: learning, training, pushing our limits and expanding our comfort zones, be they physical, mental or emotional.

What are some things you like to do to help you feel that you are growing?

To feel like I'm growing I like
to

BETTER WORLD

We all need to feel, even in a small way, that we're making our world a better place. That we're doing our part, our fair share.

For some this means keeping the world clean and contributing to the greater good. For others, it's more local: helping out in their school or in their neighborhood fills their buckets.

What are some things you like to do to help you feel that you are making the world a better place?

To make the world a better place I like to

Let's now go back to Uncle Joe (Mr. Money Bags, I like to call him).

Those three things you wanted to buy, the first ones that popped into your head, which buckets do THEY go into?

I'll go first. I did choose a beautiful island after all, and that would go in BUCKET #2, my FUN BUCKET.

We all like to have fun, right?

I also choose to give a lot of money to my friends and family. How much fun can you have by yourself?

Well, that goes into BUCKET #4, my CONNECTIONS BUCKET.

And my last one, I chose a rocket ship because... okay, no, I'm joking. Number three... I decided to give a lot of money to good causes. Which bucket does that go into? Can you guess?

That's right, BUCKET #6 for a BETTER WORLD.

Now it's your turn to go through the list and choose which buckets they fit in.

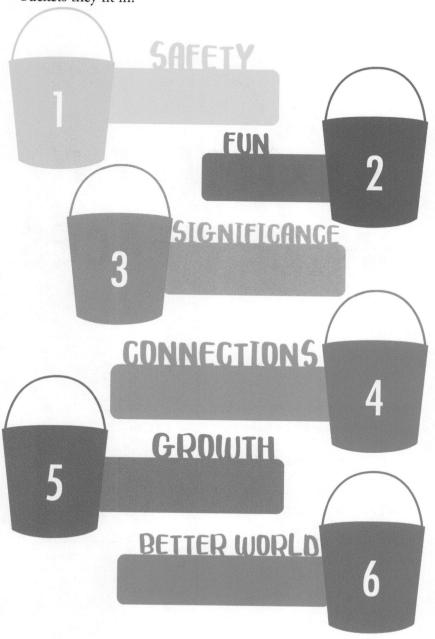

CHAPTER 5

MAXIMIZING SMILEY FACES

Now that we've answered these questions, let's take a closer look at what we do to fill our buckets.

Since we do not live alone on an island, our lives look like this.

Life's Six Buckets and 3 columns: for ME, WE, that means, you, your friends and family, and ALL or everyone else.

Let's ask ourselves a few questions to see if we can figure out where things in life go... which bucket they fit into and which box they fill.

For example, If I'm playing video games alone

It's fun.

	ME	WE	ALL
BETTER WORLD			
GROWTH			
CONNECTIONS			
SIGNIFICANCE			
FUN	✓		
SAFETY			

If I get to a new level, we could maybe... kinda, sorta say growth too but perhaps, that's a stretch.

If I'm playing video games with my buddy, and she's winning, and I'm getting upset... oh wait, that's another story, sorry.

If we're playing video games together and we're having a blast, which bucket does that go into?

	ME	WE	ALL
BETTER WORLD			
GROWTH			
CONNECTIONS		?	
SIGNIFICANCE	?		?
FUN	✓		
SAFETY			

It can fit into more than one bucket, you say? Well, you're smarter than I am, I think. And you're right.

Let's take a look.

Playing video games with my best friend fills a couple of buckets. It fills **FUN** and **CONNECTION**. It's both "ME" and "WE," isn't it? Sometimes the things we do fill more than one bucket and more than one column, and it's knowing this fact that can help us better balance our six buckets.

But wait, there's more.

Now, we can all enjoy things on our own, but science has shown over and over again that having fun with a friend or family member can be more fun and the good feeling lasts longer.

This is connected with us being humans, human beings mammals, and basically mammals have been hardwired to be social longer than we've been human.

Our brains release additional happiness chemicals when we are social, plus we tend to re-live (remember) social experiences more often.

The BUCKET CHART

When you do something for yourself, in the now or present moment, you're filling buckets 1-4 and that's 1 smiley face.

When you do something that helps your future self, filling buckets 5 or 6, give yourself 2 smiley faces.

	ME	WE	ALL
BETTER WORLD	☺ ☺		
GROWTH	☺ ☺		
CONNECTIONS	☺		
SIGNIFICANCE	☺		
FUN	☺		
SAFETY	☺		

Because humans are hardwired to be social, our happiness grows when we're doing things with or for other.

	ME	WE	ALL
BETTER WORLD	☺ ☺	☺ ☺ ☺ ☺	
GROWTH	☺ ☺	☺ ☺ ☺ ☺	
CONNECTIONS	☺	☺ ☺	
SIGNIFICANCE	☺	☺ ☺	
FUN	☺	☺ ☺	
SAFETY	☺	☺ ☺	

When we throw "the greater good" into the mix, it's even better.

	ME	WE	ALL
BETTER WORLD	☺ ☺	☺ ☺ ☺ ☺	☺ ☺ ☺ ☺ ☺ ☺ ☺ ☺
GROWTH	☺ ☺	☺ ☺ ☺ ☺	☺ ☺ ☺ ☺ ☺ ☺ ☺ ☺
CONNECTIONS	☺	☺ ☺	☺ ☺ ☺ ☺
SIGNIFICANCE	☺	☺ ☺	☺ ☺ ☺ ☺
FUN	☺	☺ ☺	☺ ☺ ☺ ☺
SAFETY	☺	☺ ☺	☺ ☺ ☺ ☺

The BUCKET CHART helps you maximize your smiley faces.

Here are three real-life scenarios: can you circle the boxes each example fills?

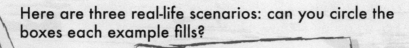

Good for me now: ☺

Good for me in the future: ☺ ☺

Good for us: ☺ ☺

Good for us in the future: ☺ ☺ / ☺ ☺

Good for all: ☺ ☺ / ☺ ☺

Good for all in the future: ☺ ☺ ☺ ☺ / ☺ ☺ ☺ ☺

You and your best friend are cooking dinner for someone you really care about. You will then share photos of the meal with family that is far away.

	ME	WE	ALL
BETTER WORLD	☺ ☺	☺ ☺ / ☺ ☺	☺ ☺ ☺ ☺ / ☺ ☺ ☺ ☺
GROWTH	☺ ☺	☺ ☺ / ☺ ☺	☺ ☺ ☺ ☺ / ☺ ☺ ☺ ☺
CONNECTIONS	☺	☺ ☺	☺ ☺ / ☺ ☺
SIGNIFICANCE	☺	☺ ☺ / ☺	☺ ☺ / ☺ ☺
FUN	(☺)	☺ ☺	☺ ☺ / ☺ ☺
SAFETY	☺	☺ ☺	☺ ☺ / ☺ ☺

You compile a "This-will-make-you-smile-playlist" of your favorite songs for your favorite person (who is over 40 or under 8 years old). You will then share the playlist online.

	ME	WE	ALL
BETTER WORLD	🙂🙂	🙂🙂 🙂	🙂🙂🙂 🙂🙂🙂
GROWTH	🙂🙂	🙂🙂 🙂	🙂🙂🙂 🙂🙂🙂
CONNECTIONS	🙂	🙂🙂	🙂🙂 🙂🙂
SIGNIFICANCE	🙂	🙂🙂	🙂🙂 🙂🙂
FUN	🙂	🙂🙂	🙂🙂 🙂🙂
SAFETY	🙂	🙂🙂	🙂🙂🙂

You and a family member swap an hour of watching TV or gaming to take a walk through a park.

	ME	WE	ALL
BETTER WORLD	🙂🙂	🙂🙂 🙂🙂	🙂🙂🙂 🙂🙂🙂
GROWTH	🙂🙂	🙂🙂 🙂🙂	🙂🙂🙂 🙂🙂🙂
CONNECTIONS	🙂	🙂🙂	🙂🙂 🙂🙂
SIGNIFICANCE	🙂	🙂🙂	🙂🙂 🙂🙂
FUN	🙂	🙂🙂	🙂🙂 🙂🙂
SAFETY	🙂	🙂🙂	🙂🙂 🙂🙂

CHAPTER 6

BUCKET NEGLECT = FEELING EMPTY

Perhaps, you're saying, I know this already.

Yes, but sometimes, life happens so fast that we forget some of our buckets aren't filling up and that's why we need to

Take care of ALL of our buckets.

Sometimes we pay attention to only one bucket or two and forget the rest. That's why it's important to know your **CORE WHYs**.

Your CORE WHYs are what you value most.

Those things you chose with Uncle Joe's money? That's right, those are your CORE WHYs.

Understanding your CORE WHYs helps you know how to take care of all your buckets throughout life.

CHAPTER 7

BALANCING YOUR BUCKETS

Our long-lost Uncle Joe had a friend, Bob.

Bob had so much money (even more than Uncle Joe, if you can believe it!), but he wasn't happy. He spent all his time trying to make more money. Does that sound familiar?

Often, someone has a lot of one thing (fame, wealth, things), but is still unhappy.

The answer is in the buckets. Some of Bob's buckets were probably empty because Bob didn't know about Life's Six Buckets and so never thought about them.

A neglected bucket is an empty bucket.

When one of your buckets is empty, guess what? You feel empty.

So, I might be happy on my big, expensive island under the sun for a while, but if my other buckets are empty, I'm going to grow sad. I'll feel empty and alone.

A fulfilled life comes from balancing ALL your buckets.

Balancing your buckets isn't hard when you know about them. Sometimes you're filling one and not paying enough attention to the others. It takes time, practice, and effort.

You don't have to fill all of them, but you do have to attend to them—pay attention and **never neglect any of them**.

Balance your buckets, and you'll balance your life.

A balanced life brings fulfillment and joy.

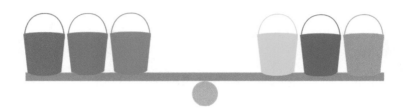

Let's start off with something easy. Something all of us can do... Let's take a few minutes each day to ask your friend or ourselves the following questions:

What did I do that filled my buckets today?

Which buckets need some attention?

When we ask ourselves these questions, we are thinking of all the good things that we have done, which is always nice, as we're paying attention to our buckets. We're not forgetting them. And maybe, hopefully, tomorrow we'll better know which bucket needs more attention.

All right, now I have to go write a thank you letter to Uncle Joe. Oh, and I need to make a phone call. I think I'm going to take a break from the island to fill some more buckets.

Good luck!

CHAPTER 8

WHY YOUR PARENTS GOT IT WRONG

When I was a kid, my father used to say, "It's ok to make mistakes, just try to not make the same mistake twice." Which I thought was fair.

Then one day, I saw an ant walking along the rim of a wide shallow bowl. The ant walked along the edge, made a full circle and kept walking. It went around the dish three times. It dawned on me that it would continue on this path because it could not see the mistake that it was making.

If you think you are right, you will continue doing what you are used to doing.

If you don't realize a mistake is being made or that there may be a better way of doing something, then you'll probably continue to do what you are used to.

Oh yeah, I blew the ant off the dish and it continued on its way.

• • • • • • • • • • •

When I was a kid growing up, life seemed simple.

To be happy, one simply needed success, fame or wealth and with one of those (it was up to you), love and friends would naturally happen.

The prescribed and desired path was to go to school and then on to university, in order to better one's chances in life. In some ways, this "study-smart-and-work-hard-for-your-goal" path was effective.

It certainly increased the individual examples of success, fame and wealth, but... not a sense of fulfillment.

In fact, the number of people who feel unhappy, hopeless and empty; including those who have achieved their goals, has increased.

Let's skip over the 'doom and gloom' of depression and opioid epidemics.

You see, "*why-people-do-what-they-do*", has always fascinated me. In my university psychology class I learned of Maslow's Pyramid and how becoming one's best self was considered the highpoint in the process of life.

However, after compiling the work of leading experts in neurology, psychology, biology, nutrition, and genetics, I now realize that:

1. What we thought would make us happy, was too simple.

2. Maslow never meant his work to be seen as a step-by-step pyramid.

Generally speaking, we are indirectly taught that life is basically a simple math problem:

A x B x C ~~other stuff~~ **= Feeling Fulfilled or NOT**

We were told to K.I.S.S. (to keep it simple sweetie/stupid).

We would insert our goals; for example A = Success. B = Wealth. C = Love (or choose fame, expertise, family, adventure... whatever you want) and away we went. Attempting to achieve our dreams/goals.

Some never actually set goals…. So they just keep plodding along.
Some never attain their goals… So they continue striving… reaching…
A rare few, manage to attain everything they set out to do.

Over time, a person's identity is highly influenced by the goals they strive for. And what typically happens, when a person considers themselves "*not-happy-enough*", is they figure they simply have not yet reached "*enough*" in their chosen pursuits.

That is easy to conclude if one has not reached their goals, but for those who HAVE reached their goals, these people then double their efforts.

Wherever they are in life… they feel somewhere in their choices A, B, C … it's 'clearly' not enough. So, if…

$$A \times B \times C \text{ other stuff} = \text{Not Fulfilled}$$

The '*logical*' step is

$$A \times B \times C \text{ other stuff} = \text{Must be Fulfilled}$$

So they work harder.

They spend even more time and effort on the path they have already spent years maybe decades on.
For those who have met with success, understandably think, I've done well so far, so "more" must be better.

If a person wants money, say they have $5,000,000 in the bank; they figure they need to make MORE money like $15,000,000… Then they will be happy.
If a person has a business, they need to make the business

bigger... Then they will be happy.

If a person wants fame, they need **more fame...Then** they will be happy.

If a person wanted a house or a car, they need a bigger house or a **better car...Then** they will be happy.

You get the point.

You just read Life's 6 Buckets, so this may sound silly or appear obvious, but to be fair...They are essentially doing what they were taught.

We were taught to **keep it simple**.
Just focus on a few things and the rest will sort itself out.

$$A \times B \times C \text{ other stuff} = \text{Fulfilled Life Score}$$

But the full equation* is

$$A \times B \times C \times D \times E \times F = \text{Fulfilled Life Score}$$

And we know that any number, no matter how big, multiplied by ZERO, is still zero.

> **A neglected bucket is an empty bucket.**
> **And when one of your buckets is empty, you feel empty**

Remember: Balance your Buckets.

*In all fairness, what else would you expect if you weren't taught the **full** equation?

You may have heard, "You have to take care of yourself before you can take care of others."

Airplanes, right?
You can't save a child if you're passed out from lack of oxygen.
And this totally applies… for crashing airplanes.
I really hope your life is not constantly in "crashing airplane" mode.

If you can avoid the extremes – the self-absorbed always 'me first' or its opposite the 'never-ever me' (aka always others), you naturally sense there is more.

Humans are mammals and mammals are social animals.
Our brains have actually been 'social', longer than they have been human.

We are hardwired to be social.

Sometimes helping others is the best way to help yourself.

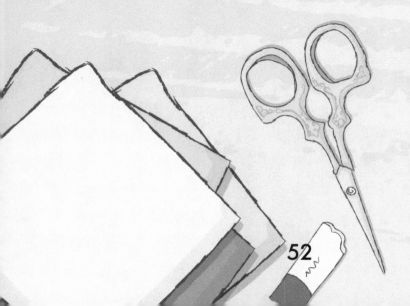

Help others
to help yourself

53

© orlysndr

CHAPTER 9

DOES LIFE'S 6 BUCKETS APPLY TO EVERYONE?

The answer is no.

Let me explain.

What we have here is a Bell Shaped Curve, which is a visual explanation of the probability of a population.
Whereby the center is considered the average/mean/median.
To the left is below average and to the right is above average

With about 95% of the population falling within 2 standard deviations. (The links explain further)

THE BELL SHAPED CURVE

Normal Distribution

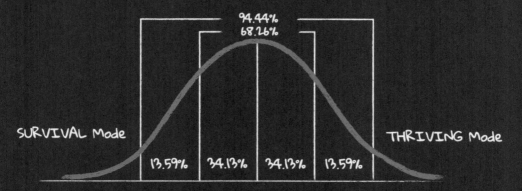

94.44%

68.26%

SURVIVAL Mode

THRIVING Mode

13.59%   34.13%   34.13%   13.59%

There is a small percentage of the population, to the far left, that is in Survival Mode.
Anywhere where basic safety and survival is a constant threat… war, famine, violence.
This part of the population is focused on *staying alive*, not on living a fulfilled life.

On the other side of the curve is a small population that is thriving in a particular area and they are motivated to becoming the world's greatest … something.
They are laser-beam focused on a very specific goal.
And at this stage in their life, it is that pursuit, which dominates their life.

Aside from these 2 extremes, I believe everyone within the 95% can benefit from the Fulfillment Source Code's 6 Buckets.
Hopefully, taking everyone from Survive to Thrive.

And just a side note, you don't need to agree with everything to get something out of the Foundation Source Code.

LIFE'S 6 BUCKETS ~~WORKBOOK~~ PLAYBOOK

You know we have the same WHYs… We all need/want:

1. Safety - to feel safe and secure.

2. Fun – to have fun and feel good.

3. Significance - to feel like we matter.

4. Connections - to feel loved/connected with our friends and family

5. Growth –to feel we are becoming a better version of ourselves

6. Better World - to feel, even in a small way, that we're making our world a better place.

And I think it' safe to say, that you know that different people can enjoy different WHATs to fill their WHYs. What is fun for you may not be fun for others.

But… can you see how it is possible for 2 people to enjoy the same WHAT, for different WHYs?

For example, traveling:

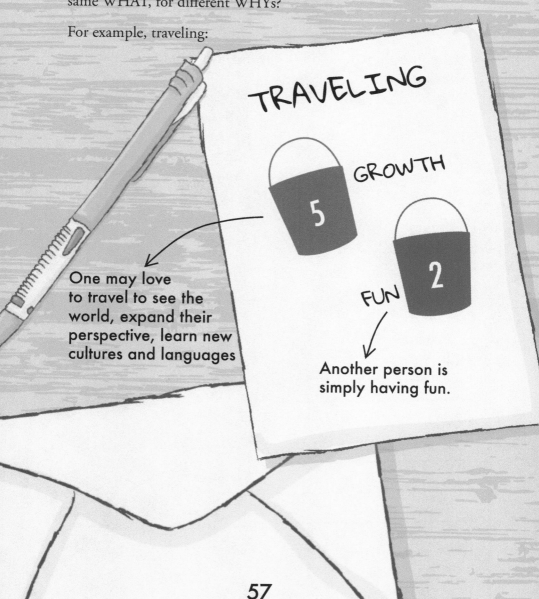

TRAVELING

GROWTH

5

FUN

2

One may love to travel to see the world, expand their perspective, learn new cultures and languages

Another person is simply having fun.

Same WHY different WHATS

vs.

Same WHAT different WHYS

Can you think of other activities that could fill multiple buckets?

Activity:

_____

Buckets Filled:

_____

_____

_____

Activity:

_____

Buckets Filled:

_____

_____

_____

Activity:

_____

Buckets Filled:

_____

_____

_____

Activity:

_____

Buckets Filled:

_____

_____

_____

CReate YOUR 6-Bucket Sentence

A great way to remember Life's Six Buckets is to have some fun creating your OWN sentence using the first letter of each bucket.

Safety – Fun – Significance – Connections – Growth – Better World

S-F-S-C-G-BW

Sam Finds Sophie Can Grow Big Watermelons

_____

_____

_____

_____

_____

_____

_____

The Fulfillment Source Code and WHY it came from

Hi.

My name is Sam Goodman.

I am a dad, a serial entrepreneur and now an interactive storyteller.

I believe everyone wants to become their best selves, be happy, and lead a fulfilled life, but unfortunately.... we simply don't learn those "skills" in school. And yet, the tools to do so are out there.

I believe this so much that I've dedicated years curating the world's leading experts and compacted them into a 20-hour course full of cool ideas a 10-year-old finds fun to learn.

The course has been tested and is kid and parent-approved. In the spring of 2018 the Montessori School of Beijing, one of China's most innovative schools, provided the complete Fulfillment Source Code to its 6th-grade class and the response was awesome! In 2019, the course was given to two 6th-grade classes in the Western Academy of Beijing.

Our Mission: educate and empower kids to lead a fulfilled life.

Our Goal: provide the FSC course to kids everywhere.

This book is only about one-third of the first class of the FSC course.

The course contains the fundamental evidence-based WHYs, humans need to better their chances at leading a fulfilled life. It's everything I wish I knew when I was a 10.

The latest in neurology, biology, psychology, genetics, and nutrition

The Fulfillment Source Code is not aiming to be a traditional "module" to be taught. It requires active participation, like a choose-your-own-adventure, with each child as the hero of their own story.

Some of the ABC's of the Fulfillment Source Code

A **WHY** their brain is better suited for life 50,000 years ago

B **WHY** pain and fear used to be your brain's BFF

C **WHY** your brain wants to conserve energy

D **WHY** 95% of your brain activity happens automatically & unconsciously

E **WHY** your thoughts can physically change your brain

F **WHY** conscious thinking is your brain's 2nd mode and 2nd favorite mode of operation.

G **HOW** cool it is to know the various ways the brain works

H **HOW** the brain is like computer hardware and the mind is like computer software and yet so much more

I **WHY** your mind can literally change the physical brain

J **WHY** repeating teeny-tiny steps can lead to immense change (positive or negative)

K **HOW** focused thought is hard, powerful, flawed and easily influenced/manipulated

L **WHY** more sleep is one of their most underutilized tools for learning

M **HOW** sleep makes you a more creative problem solver

N **HOW** they decide to play a few games, can forever change their life

O **HOW** sticking your thumb on your forehead increases your test scores by 5% (Ok... That's not true. But if it were, you would totally be doing it. This proves a point from class 1)

P **WHY** the road to life fulfilment is not about singular goals, but about balancing 6 'buckets'

Q **WHY** learning that there are as many neurons in their gut, as in a cat's brain is not only awesome, but incredibly important

R **WHY** learning a few words in Latin is both cool and can profoundly change your life.

S **WHY** screen time can be addictive and HOW it happens

T **WHY** a few minutes of screen time right before bed, can really screw up your brain (and therefore a whole lot about your life)

U **WHY** cramming before an exam is a horrible strategy

V **WHY** learning all this in Grade 5/6 is the optimal time in their life

W **WHY** their brain rewires itself in puberty and all the ways that affects them

X **HOW** refined sugar is affecting so much more than their teeth: their body, their gut and their brain

Y **HOW** your brain reacts to love and processes death

Z **WHY** teaching all the above (and more) to their parents actually helps them learn better

SOURCES of the Fulfillment Source Code Content

Well... some of them

Harvard, Princeton, Stanford, Oxford, and Wharton Alum & Professors (**John Ratey, Angela Duckworth, Tal Ben-Shahar, Daniel Gilbert, Carol Dweck**)

Nobel Prize Winner (**Daniel Kahneman**)

3 time Winner of the Science in Society Journalism Award (**Gary Taubes**)

Dean of the Rotman School of Management at the University of Toronto (**Roger Martin**)

Director of the Brain Center for Applied Learning Research at Seattle Pacific University & Professor of Bioengineering at the University of Washington School of Medicine (**John Medina**)

Professor and Social Cognitive Neuroscience Lab Director at UCLA (**Matthew Lieberman**)

Professor and Chair of the Department of Neurology at the Perelman School of Medicine, University of Pennsylvania (**Dr. Frances E. Jensen**)

Distinguished Professor of Psychology and Management at Claremont Graduate University. He is the former head of the department of psychology (**Mihaly Csikszentmihalyi**)

Founder one of the world's largest hedge funds. (**Ray Dalio**)

References

99.9% Genetically Identical

1.   U.S. Centers for Disease Control, www.cdc.gov/genomics/public/faq.htm

Life's Why, How, & What's

1.   Sinek, Simon. *Start with Why: How Great Leaders Inspire Everyone to Take Action.* Portfolio/Penguin, 2013.

2.   Christakis, N. A., & Fowler, J. H. (2018). *Connected: The surprising power of our social networks and how they shape our lives: How your friends friends friends affect everything you feel, think, and do.* Vancouver, B.C.: Langara College.

3.   Lieberman, Matthew D. University Of California Los Angeles. *Social - Why Our Brains Are Wired to Connect.* Oxford University Press, 2015.

Life's 6 Buckets

1.   Maslow's hierarchy of needs. (2019, May 28). Retrieved from https://en.wikipedia.org/wiki/Maslow's_hierarchy_of_needs

2.   6 Core Human Needs by Anthony Robbins. (n.d.). Retrieved from https://www.habitsforwellbeing.com/6-core-human-needs-by-anthony-robbins/

3.   Winter, Theo. "Maslow's Hierarchy: Separating Fact From Fiction." *Main*, 8 Dec. 2017, www.td.org/insights/maslows-hierarchy-separating-fact-from-fiction.

Life's 6 Buckets Chart

1. Ben-Shahar, T. (2012). *Happier: Can you learn to be happy.* S.l.: McGrawHill.

2. "The Neurochemicals of Happiness." *Psychology Today*, Sussex Publishers, www.psychologytoday.com/us/blog/the-athletes-way/201211/the-neurochemicals-happiness.

3. "The Helper's High." *Greater Good*, greatergood.berkeley.edu/article/item/the_helpers_high.

4. Davis, Jeanie Lerche. "The Science of Good Deeds." *WebMD*, www.webmd.com/balance/features/science-good-deeds.

5. Kahneman, D. (2015). *Thinking, fast and slow. New York: Farrar, Straus and Giroux.*

6. Doidge, N. (2017). *The brain that changes itself: Stories of personal triumph from the frontiers of brain science.* Strawberry Hills, NSW: ReadHowYouWant.

7. Diener, E., & Seligman, M. E. (2004). *Beyond money: Toward an economy of well-beeing.* Malden: Blackwell Publ.

8. Ratey, John J., and Eric Hagerman. *Spark: the Revolutionary New Science of Exercise and the Brain.* Little, Brown and Company, 2013.

9. "Dopamine, Smartphones & You: A Battle for Your Time." *Science in the News,* 27 Feb. 2019, sitn.hms.harvard.edu/flash/2018/dopamine-smartphones-battle-time/.

10. Palaus, M., et al (2017). Neural basis of video gaming: A systematic review. *Frontiers of Human Neuroscience*, 11, article 248.

Finally, thank you to all FSC Supporters:

A Kahn, Ali, B Horst, Beijing Bjorn, Ben, Big D., Clan Kinlough, Coop-shoots, Cynthia, D Chong, Dave!!!, Dirk, Eli, Eyee, Faye, Gentleman James, Guy, Hersh, Sara and Lil' Dan, Irene, Izzy's Dad, J Courville, J Riel, Jethro, Julia, K Lam, Marc, Sunny and Bowie, Mr. Lepa, Mr. Seto, my favorite Mendels, my sister from another mister, N Zhou, R Smolen, Reed, Roberta & Ted, Rory, Sig, Sophie's God-mom, Spambeano, Su, Tenacious D, the Beer Family from Germany, the Beijing Robinsons, the Colby's, the Furers, the Gagnon-Lius, the Grammer-Granma, the Kalles Family, the Kurtzig Clan, the Lyons, the McColl Family, the Orangey-ist Orange, the Southshield's Clan, the Toronto Gaums, the Westers, Ykceb Namdoog, and Zsuzsanna.

CPSIA information can be obtained
at www.ICGtesting.com
Printed in the USA
LVHW071936141019
634123LV00001B/57/P